What Was It Like During Christmas in the 80s?

A Journal to Revisit and Share the 80s Holiday Spirit

~ Riya Aarini ~

This book belongs to '80s kid

NORTH POLE
SANTA CLAUS
AIR MAIL
NORTH POLE

_____

_____

Contents

Merry Christmas

Welcome to Your '80s Christmases!

Christmas in the 1980s brings back fond memories for many, perhaps because it belonged to the carefree days of their childhood or because an '80s Christmas truly was distinct.

After all, people braved the snow and crowds to browse the festive malls in person, shopping for just the right holiday presents—unlike today's fast-paced holiday seasons, where virtually everything is purchased online with one click and received in the blink of an eye. In fact, shipping in the '80s took a month or more; gift purchases had to be planned strategically to arrive in the nick of time!

But the generous spirit of Christmas endures, regardless of the decade. Santa Claus still wears his bright red suit and fluffy beard, delivers presents based on his Naughty and Nice lists, and inspires all-around cheer. People continue Christmas traditions, like attending holiday shows and listening to unforgettable Christmas classics.

Return to your childhood Christmases in this guided journal, which takes you back to the specialness of the '80s holiday seasons. Sip a mug of hot cocoa by the blazing fire and scribble in your answers for a cozy evening of nostalgia. Share the completed journal with loved ones, so they glean how you celebrated Christmas in the exuberant '80s!

Christmas Tree

Did the magic of Christmas officially start once you put up the tree?

How soon before Christmas did your family set up the holiday tree?

Did your family prefer a live or an artificial Christmas tree?

If a live tree, how did you obtain it? A farm, the woods?

If an artificial tree, where did you get it from?

In what part of the home did your family put up the holiday tree?

Did you help decorate the tree? If so, how did you embellish it? Garlands, silver tinsel, strings of lights?

If tinsel was a part of your tree decorations, did you go all out covering the tree (and home) with the sparkly strands?

Who held the honor of topping the Christmas tree with the star?

How long after Christmas did your family keep the tree up?

What did you do with the Christmas tree once the holiday season ended?

Ornaments

Describe a cherished holiday ornament.

Did your family hang holiday ornaments passed down from prior generations? If so, describe one and its significance.

Did you craft holiday ornaments?

If you handmade Christmas ornaments, express how it felt to hang them on the tree.

Holiday Decorations

How did you decorate your home's exterior for Christmas?

Did your family create handmade Christmas lawn decorations? If so, describe one.

Did your family take scenic drives through neighborhoods to admire homes lit up for Christmas? Describe the sights and your sense of awe.

Ugly Christmas
Sweaters

Ugly Christmas sweaters grew to be a cultural phenomenon in the '80s. Glitter, exaggerated patterns, garish colors, pompoms, and sequins made bold fashion statements, and–combined with Christmas motifs–ugly sweaters became the perfect style choice during the flashy '80s.

Did you wear ugly Christmas sweaters? If so, describe one.

Was it handmade or purchased?

Did you find ugly Christmas sweaters charming?

Did you feel the sweaters' ugliness was a part of their appeal?

Did the festive ugly sweaters evoke a spirit of playfulness?

Describe a memorable reaction to your ugly Christmas sweater.

Christmas Shopping

Did you scour through holiday print catalogs to find Christmas gifts you liked to receive or give?

Did you write a Christmas wish list, noting the catalog page numbers?

How early did you start Christmas shopping in the '80s?

How much time did you or your family spend at the malls shopping for Christmas gifts?

How crowded did the malls get during the holiday shopping seasons?

How many times did your family circle the mall parking lot to find a parking space?

How impressive were the toy stores/sections in the '80s?

Did the mall go to great lengths to decorate for Christmas in the '80s? Describe the sights and sounds.

Did bands play Christmas music live at the malls? If so, did you enjoy the experience?

Did the malls hold shows with animatronic Christmas figures? If so, how spectacular were they?

Describe a mall-related fiasco (like splitting up or getting lost in the sea of shoppers).

How well did you time gift purchases to receive them before Christmas, since shipping took several weeks in the '80s?

Despite the frenzy and crowds, did mall shopping in the '80s inspire a sense of comfort and community—unlike shopping online today?

Did you enjoy the hustle and bustle of Christmas shopping in the '80s?

Did your Christmas gifts come with stories, such as having to drive fifty miles through snow and ice, only to find the store had none left in stock? If so, tell one story.

Christmas Gifts

Name five dream Christmas gifts you received in the '80s.

_____

_____

_____

_____

_____

Did you ever receive a lump of coal? If so, why?

Describe a handmade Christmas gift you received in the '80s.

List three gifts you found in your Christmas stockings.

_____

_____

_____

Did you ever ask Santa for a gift and didn't receive it? How did you justify that?

Did you ever find receipts for the Christmas gifts you received, introducing doubts about the existence of Santa Claus?

Did you ever catch your parents sneaking gifts under the tree on Christmas Eve?

If so, what emotions ran through you?

Explain how you caught them. A camcorder, in person?

Did receiving Christmas presents in the '80s hold greater meaning than today? If so, why?

Do you think people gave fewer Christmas gifts during the '80s, making the exchanges more exquisite experiences?

Santa Claus

How old were you when you first learned about Santa Claus?

Who explained Santa Claus to you?

What emotions ran through you when you discovered Santa brought toys and joys every Christmas?

How magical did Santa feel to you?

Did you visit Santa? If so, where? Common places included the mall, Christmas-themed amusement parks, and winter wonderlands.

What did you think of Santa upon meeting him?

.

Did you take home a photo of Santa and you? If so, describe the photo.

Do you still have this photo?

Did you write letters to Santa Claus? If so, what did you ask for?

Did you mail the letter to the North Pole? If so, describe from where you mailed it (ie, home, school, post office).

Did you wait up on Christmas Eve to get a peek at Santa leaving gifts under the Christmas tree? If so, how late did you stay up?

Did you ever catch Santa in action?

Until what age did you believe in Santa Claus?

Explain how you learned the truth about Santa Claus.

Did your world shatter?

Santa's Elves

Did you believe in Santa's elves?

Until what age did the fascination for the toy-making elves continue?

Santa's Reindeer

How did you learn about Santa's reindeer? Christmas TV specials, holiday stories, Christmas songs, holiday décor?

Growing up, who was your favorite reindeer? Why?

Did you ever stay out on Christmas Eve, gazing at the sky to look for Santa's team of flying reindeer?

What did you believe gave Santa's reindeer the ability to fly? Magic dust, belief in Santa, special food, or something else?

Holiday Books

Name your three favorite childhood Christmas books.

_____

_____

_____

If your family read Christmas stories together, describe the storytime environment. Next to the warmth of a crackling fireplace, while cozily tucked in bed?

What holiday story held the most meaning for you, and why?

Who were your most beloved characters? What about them appealed to you?

Christmas Poems

Clement Clark Moore's "A Visit from St. Nicholas," also known as "'Twas the Night Before Christmas," with its snappy rhythm and cheer, left a memorable impression on many.

What Christmas poem captivated you most as an '80s kid?

Did you recite this poem as a Christmas tradition?

Christmas Movies

Top holiday movie picks included
1983: "A Christmas Story"
1988: "Ernest Saves Christmas"
1989: "National Lampoon's Christmas Vacation"

Name your favorite '80s Christmas movies.

Which movie best described Christmas in the '80s?

Where did you watch Christmas movies? At home on a VCR, in the theater, elsewhere?

With whom did you watch Christmas movies?

Did you rewatch Christmas movies in the '80s? If so, which ones, and how often?

If the nostalgia is strong, do you rewatch your best-loved childhood Christmas movies today?

Christmas TV Specials

Well-liked Christmas specials included "A Charlie Brown Christmas," "A Garfield Christmas," and "A Muppet Family Christmas."

What were your favorite Christmas TV specials in the '80s?

Did you refer to the "TV Guide" schedule to ensure you didn't miss the specials—since they aired once annually?

Did your family watch Christmas specials together? If so, what lasting memories did those times create?

Christmas Carols

Did you sing Christmas carols in the '80s? If so, with whom? Family, choir, professional carolers, Girl Scout troop?

Did you go house-to-house singing carols?

List three beloved Christmas carols.

_____

_____

_____

Christmas Music

Tunes that topped the charts included
1981: "Christmas Wrapping," the Waitresses
1984: "Last Christmas," Wham!
1985: "Merry Christmas Everyone," Shakin' Stevens

List your '80s Christmas song picks.

Christmas Theater

Visiting the theater was a popular holiday tradition during the '80s. Theatrical productions with themes of hope, goodwill, and peace were must-sees, bringing people together in the spirit of Christmas.

Did you see "The Nutcracker"? If so, describe the sentiments the classical ballet inspired.

Did you see an adaptation of "A Christmas Carol"? If so, where?

Holiday Train Rides

Did you take holiday train rides in the '80s? If so, where?

Did the rides instill a sense of wonder and magic in you?

Describe how the holiday train was decorated.

How memorable were the holiday train rides?

Holiday Sleigh Rides

Did you take holiday sleigh rides through the snow?

Describe the enchantment of being pulled through the snow.

Sensory Experiences

Christmas in the '80s conjured up distinct aromas, sights, sounds, feels, and tastes.

Aromas

What were some unique scents of Christmas? The smell of pine needles, cloves and nutmeg from freshly baked gingerbread cookies...

Sights

What were some of the unforgettable sights of Christmas in the '80s? The soft glow from holiday lights, the decorated street posts...

Sounds

What sounds of '80s Christmases do you recall? The jingle of bells, the crunching of boots through the snow...

Feels

Describe the unforgettable feels of Christmas in the '80s. The cozy, oversized holiday sweaters, the biting cold...

Tastes

List the irresistible flavors of Christmas in the '80s. Peppermint candy canes, mint chocolates...

Flashes from the '80s Christmases Past

Flashes from the '80s
Christmases Past

Gingerbread Houses

Did you build gingerbread houses as a youth?

If so, did your family make the dough from scratch?

What '80s candies did you use to decorate the gingerbread houses?

Window Displays

Elaborately decorated window displays were a big part of the '80s Christmas seasons and attracted countless shoppers into department stores.

Did your family stroll past storefronts to admire the holiday window displays?

If so, describe one window display that stood out.

Christmas Vacations

How did you spend Christmas vacations in the '80s?

Did your family travel? If so, to what holiday destinations?

Christmas Plays

Did you participate in a Christmas play?

If so, name a favorite character you played.

Describe a memorable costume.

Holiday Cookies

Popular Christmas cookies included candy cane cookies, shortbread cookies, and classic thumbprint cookies. The tasty morsels symbolized thankfulness, sharing, and togetherness.

Describe your favorite store-bought holiday cookies.

Did your family bake holiday cookies? If so, was it a family holiday tradition?

Christmas Eve

How did you spend Christmas Eve in the '80s?

Did you feel excitement, longing, or anticipation on Christmas Eve, knowing the next morning you'd wake up to new gifts?

Christmas Day

How did you spend Christmas Day in the '80s?

Did you follow any Christmas traditions? If so, describe one.

Christmas Breakfasts
or Brunches

Did your family prepare Christmas breakfasts or brunches? If so, what dishes did they whip up?

Describe one of your best holiday breakfast memories from the '80s.

Christmas Dinners

What were your favorite Christmas dinner menu items?

Did you prefer homemade stuffing and gravy over boxed or store-bought variations?

Did your family hold a Christmas potluck or buffet? What foods did friends and family bring?

Describe the factors that went into making Christmas dinners memorable. Delicious food, camaraderie?

Christmas Desserts

Festive treats in the '80s included Yule log cakes, fruitcakes, Christmas tiramisu, and gelatin molds.

What holiday desserts did you look forward to?

What was your opinion of fruitcakes, which received a bad rap in the '80s?

Did you regift the notoriously dry fruitcakes in the '80s?

If so, how many times did the fruitcakes pass through your social circle before being discarded?

Christmas Parties

Did your school throw Christmas parties? If so, what holiday activities did you enjoy?

Did your family hold Christmas parties? If so, describe the festive '80s outfits.

Long-Distance
Holiday Greetings

The cost of long-distance calls in the '80s averaged $0.30 to $0.50 per minute. During peak hours, like Christmas, the price rose exponentially higher.

Did your family make long-distance telephone calls on Christmas?

How expensive did the calls get?

How long or short did you keep the calls?

Did you ship Christmas presents internationally? If so, how long did they take to reach?

Social Interactions

Do you feel people interacted more authentically during Christmas in the '80s (when smartphones didn't consume their attention)?

Did you feel a special bond with others, even strangers, on Christmas?

White Christmases

Did you wake up to white Christmases in the '80s?

If snow was abundant in your region, what winter activities did you enjoy? Building snowmen, sledding, making snow angels, building snow forts, snowball fights?

How magical did it feel to drive through Christmas snow?

Charities and Volunteering

Did you or your family give to charity during Christmas in the '80s? If so, to which one?

Did you volunteer during the holidays in the '80s? If so, where?

Christmas Intangibles

On Christmas Day in the '80s, shops closed, and employees welcomed the opportunity to spend time with loved ones.

Did you consider Father Time on your side during Christmas in the '80s? In other words, did time move at a slower pace, allowing you to savor the moments of the season?

Did you feel greater anticipation during Christmas in the '80s (compared to today where nearly everything, from toys to movies, is available on-demand)?

Did you awake early on Christmas morning to an incredibly moving peace and quiet?

Was Christmas simpler in the '80s? What made it so?

Did Christmas in the '80s hold greater sanctity?

What did you appreciate most about Christmas in the '80s?

Describe your most unforgettable '80s Christmas.

What was the true meaning of Christmas for you in the '80s?

Here's to an Unforgettable '80s Christmas!

While technology improves, from the endless options for holiday lights to the brilliant luminaries for the front yard, the spirit of Christmas remains unchanged. As it goes, some things are too good for improvement–like the joyful feelings of community when singing carols and spending time in the company of loved ones, immersed in the distinct sights, sounds, and feels of the holiday seasons. Eras change, but Christmas joy is timeless!

More Flashes from the '80s Christmases Past

More Flashes from the '80s Christmases Past

Books in the
What Was It Like series

What Was It Like Growing Up in the 70s?
A Journal to Revisit and Share the Groovy 70s

What Was It Like Growing Up in the 80s?
A Journal to Revisit and Share the Totally Awesome 80s

What Was It Like Fooding in the 80s?
A Journal to Revisit and Share 80s Totally Tubular Eats

What Was It Like Growing Up in the 90s?
A Journal to Revisit and Share the Rad 90s

What Was It Like During Christmas in the 90s?
A Journal to Revisit and Share the 90s Holiday Vibe

What Was It Like Marrying in the 90s?
A Journal (for Her) to Revisit and Share 90s Wedding
Magic